LIBYA: A FUTURE ARAB DEMOCRACY

Dubbed the Arab Spring, beginning in early 2010 a wave of Muslim populations across the North African coast and Persian Gulf as well as in Syria have rebelled against their long standing rulers. They are demanding more from their governments. The people seek more responsiveness to their concerns, more fairness, less corruption from their officials, and more jobs. They seek justice and opportunity. To date actual regime change has occurred in Tunisia, Egypt, Libya, and Yemen but the ultimate outcome of the uprisings is rendered uncertain by the still to be seen capabilities and direction of the newly formed transitional governments. Egypt, a cradle of civilization, possessing the Suez Canal, a border with Israel and the largest population in the Middle East, remains the most strategically significant State in the region. Libya's geography, vast energy resources, highly developed population, and close ties to Europe may, however, render it a more promising candidate for establishing a lasting democracy.

Of all the uprising States, in Libya alone did Western military intervention significantly tip the balance of power and lead to the defeat of an Arab regime at the hands of the (NATO supported) National Transition Counsel (NTC). Although Libya is the latest Arab government to fall, Gadhafi was the first national leader to be removed by force with Western military assistance. The U.S. and its Allies believed that the failure to protect civilians called for in UN Resolutions 1970 and 1973 would create a humanitarian crisis and a flood of refugees into neighboring countries and Europe. Tunisia and Egypt, struggling to maintain stability and form new governments, could ill afford to assist tens of thousands of displaced Libyans.[1] The U.S. and NATO also realized that failure to intervene and stop the indiscriminate killing of civilians would also severely degrade their credibility and the legitimacy of the U.N.[2]

U.S. intervention in Libya was driven foremost by U.N. Security Council Resolution 1973 authorizing the protection of Libyan civilians by "all necessary measures, notwithstanding paragraph 9 of resolution 1970 (2011), to protect civilians and civilian populated areas under threat of attack in the Libyan Arab Jamahiriya, including Benghazi, while excluding a foreign occupation force of any form on any part of Libyan territory." The U.S. believed that it could protect Libyan civilians without the use of U.S. ground forces and at minimal risk to U.S. military forces.[3] U.S. actions would be sanctioned by the United Nations, and conducted exclusively as part of a broad coalition. Libya's previous State sponsorship of terrorism, including the Lockerbie, Scotland and Berlin attacks that killed U.S. citizens made military intervention against the Gadhafi regime easier to support domestically.[4]

Gadhafi himself stiffened international resolve by using a degree of military force against his own people that other governments had not employed, presenting a case for humanitarian intervention that set uneasy precedents. Having the most at stake in Libya, Britain and France, aided by Qatar and the United Arab Emirates, conducted the bulk of combat operations.[5] The United States, having less in the game, participated primarily through its leadership role in NATO planning and coordination efforts rather than through direct military action.[6]

A humanitarian catastrophe in Libya would not only flood Tunisia and Egypt with displaced Libyans but would inundate Europe with a quarter million persons seeking refuge. This would swell the tens of thousands of North Africans already in Europe as a result of the earlier Arab Spring uprisings. Further, Libya is the largest supplier of both Crude Oil as well as Natural Gas to Italy, as well as a major supplier to France.[7] Consequently Libya's major European and American trading partners have a great deal at stake in continued Libyan stability.

The U.S. believes that Libya touches its national interest mainly as it relates to NATO solidarity and counterterrorism concerns. The U.S. considers that it should therefore support NATO's activities and take other actions to prevent Libya from becoming a failed state. In the U.S. view, Libya must be inhospitable to terrorism and retain control of its borders to prevent the movement of terrorists and weapons into or out of the country and avoid potentially destabilizing the region.[8] Known Libyan chemical weapons that have not already been destroyed must also secured.[9]

It is vitally important that Libya continue to be a major energy supplier to world markets and expand its current production capacity. Oil and Gas exports are the primary source of Government revenue and central to funding essential services, employment, and reconstruction. Expanding Libyan capacity will be useful in both promoting stability internally as well as meeting growing global demand.

After over forty years of dictatorship, Libya is now led by a National Transition Council (NTC) that emerged mostly from the eastern city of Benghazi under the leadership of Dr. Mahmoud Jibril, a U.S. educated economist. Following the fall of Tripoli, Dr Jibril announced his resignation and another U.S. educated technocrat was elected to lead the governing counsel. Dr. Abdel-Rahim El Keib, a dual U.S. – Libyan citizen, spent roughly thirty years in the U.S. after attaining a PhD from North Carolina State University and then teaching many years at the University of Alabama.

Dr. Keib has long been opposed to the Gadhafi regime and joined the Libyan resistance in 1976 after leaving the country.[10] His colleagues from the University of Alabama describe Dr. Keib as a pious yet moderate Muslim that lead the Muslim community in Tuscaloosa, Alabama. After the attacks of September 11, 2001 Dr. Keib frequently participated in inter-faith dialog promoting understanding and reconciliation between Christians and Muslims.[11] At the first press conference after his selection as Prime Minister, Dr Keib spoke in English, commending Libyan forces, thanking NATO for their support, and asking for time to formulate a way forward. He was clearly looking to reassure Western Governments of his commitment to retaining close ties.

The challenges facing Dr Keib and the successful transformation of Libya are daunting. Forty two years of military dictatorship leaves the nation with limited institutions on which to build its future. There were no political parties prior to the uprising, the military is fractured, and there is no labor or trade unions or associations. Under Gadhafi, Libya was purged of any organization or association that could potentially become a threat to his power[12]. This leaves little to build on other than tribal and religious based organizations, neither of which is ideal for founding a new democracy.

The reestablishment of essential services (water, sewer, and electricity), rule of law, and security will be central elements in the Libyan transition. Much like Baghdad was the center of gravity for Iraq, Tripoli is the cultural as well as political capital of Libya. During the fighting, natural gas, electricity, and water supply were disrupted to large sections of the city. Rapid restoration of these services will be essential to building support for the new regime and restoring rule of law. If Tripoli suffers the same fuel and electricity shortages that plague Baghdad, the population may blame the fledgling transition government for their misery. The new Libyan Government will be judged by its progress measured not by legislative action but by tangible indicators such as supply of electricity, regular trash collection, and availability of oil and gas.[13]

One of the significant challenges associated with restoration of essential services is the loss of highly skilled Libyan and expatriate workers that have either been expelled or fled the instability. The NTC will need to encourage the return of highly skilled expatriate Libyans and the one million foreign workers that have fled the country.[14] This point is underscored by the return of the long absent Dr. Abdel-Rahim El Keib to assume the role of Prime Minister of the National Transition Counsel. As the new Government of Libya must create and recreate many institutions from scratch, the degree of return of its academic and industrial elite will greatly influence its success or failure.

Fortunately, the Libyan Police Forces remained relatively intact throughout the conflict and are able to resume law enforcement in many areas of the country. However, as in both Iraq and Afghanistan, large numbers of weapons, both heavy and personal are still in the hands of militias. The heavily armed and poorly trained men could pose a significant challenge to the new Government. Without the militias the uprising would not have been possible. However sovereign states must maintain a monopoly on the legitimate use of violence within their borders, and armed gangs of questionable discipline and loyalty are unhealthy for any state. As was the case in Iraq, reconciliation between militias that fought against the previous regime and its Military is proving very difficult as each side is highly suspicious of the other. Without a strong and, most importantly, recognized National police force, reconciliation and reconstruction will likely flounder due to a lack of security and rule of law.[15]

The rapid establishment of a highly trusted and elite Libyan security force will be critical to rapidly securing the new government as well as its numerous weapon stockpiles. Like Saddam Hussein, Gadhafi amassed huge amounts of conventional arms including advanced anti aircraft missiles, anti vehicle and anti personnel mines, tanks, artillery pieces, aircraft, and literal tons of individual and crew served weapons. Libya has never established training and maintenance programs that would allow it to effectively utilize its vast arsenal; securing the remaining stores will be important to the future safety and stability in Libya and the region.[16]

In the near future there is likely to be little external threat to Libya due to the effectiveness of the African Union, United Nations, and NATO at discouraging interstate violence.[17] Correspondingly, the greatest threat lies internally with the proliferation of weapons throughout the population, remnant rebel militias, and turmoil as a new government is forming. There is little need for external defense enhancement which can easily be provided by the African Union or NATO forces, but a great need for the strengthening of the police forces and ability to provide rule of law. The police forces under the previous regime were effective but often brutal, complicating their reconciliation with the new government.

In the past Libya pursued weapons of mass destruction (WMD) to include chemical as well as nuclear weapons. The previously known chemical munitions sites are purportedly under control; however reports of additional and previously unknown caches are coming forward. Rumors of unsecured raw uranium as well as stockpiles of

6

"yellow cake" nuclear material are surfacing. Positive control and elimination of WMD and its components are essential not only to the future Libyan government but to the world as well.

The WMD programs as well as the vast stores of conventional weapons were all funded by oil revenues. Libya possesses the largest reserves in Africa, currently estimated in excess of forty six billion barrels. This is among the ten largest reserves in the world. The majority of the known reserves and 90% of current production come from the area known as the Sirte basin in eastern Libya near the city of Benghazi. The discovery of additional reserves is highly probable as vast areas of Libya remain unexplored in the area of energy resources.[18]

The embargos placed on Libya in the 1980's and 90's due to their state sponsorship of terrorism had dire effects on the oil infrastructure. Libyan fields are in need of upgrading after years of neglect, but are estimated to hold vast quantities of high quality crude. The crude oil produced in Libya is low in sulfur and is among the best in the world for making transportation fuels. The Bayside Refinery located just South of New York City imports almost all of its crude from Libya to produce the Gasoline and Diesel that supplies New York City. According to refinery executives, the high wax content in the Libyan Crude allows for a very efficient refining process with high yields and little waste.[19] Libya's current oil production is in excess of one million barrels a day and should increase to over two million barrels in the next three to five years. At its height Libya was producing over three million barrels of oil per day, a production goal that the National Oil Company states it can achieve within 5 years[20].

Located on the Mediterranean Sea, Libya is close to the European markets that are the destination of 85% of its oil exports. In partnership with Colony Capital based in the United States, the Libyan government owns thousands of service stations in Italy, Egypt, and other African nations. Italy is currently Libya's largest trading partner and combined with France accounts for the majority of Libyan exports. A significant piece of infrastructure that literally ties Libya and Italy is the Greenstream Natural Gas Pipeline. The Greenstream pipeline runs for over 350 miles under the Mediterranean connecting Libya with Italy and supplying in excess of 11 Billion cubic meters of natural gas to Europe.

The Greenstream is currently the largest pipeline connecting the two continents and a vital source of energy for Italy and revenue for Libya. The pipeline connects European markets with a reliable source of fuel that was previously difficult for Libya to capture and utilize. The gas supplies coming from Africa provide Europe with an alternative to the supplies coming from Russia that are often used as a strategic bargaining tool and threatened to be cut off. In addition, the Greenstream Pipeline expansion is being planned to connect the vast quantities of Natural Gas currently being flared off in Nigeria with the Libyan line and piped to the European markets.

Capturing the Nigerian Natural Gas and building a pipeline to connect with the Trans Mediterranean line is not only good for the environment, as Nigeria literally burns off 20% of the Gas produced in the world, but excellent for the region. Prior to going under the Mediterranean Sea, the pipeline would traverse Northern Nigeria, the land locked and poverty stricken nation of Niger, and Libya. The economic futures of Europe and Africa would be literally connected, much needed jobs and revenue would be created and trade and stability supported along a route that is now mostly arid desert.

In addition to vast oil and gas reserves, Libya also has some of the best refining capacity in North Africa with five facilities capable of refining 400,000 barrels a day. This vastly exceeds Libya's internal demands and provides a lucrative export. Libya's refining sector was also greatly impacted by former UN sanctions but can be upgraded relatively quickly to provide additional gasoline and other light products to the African and nearby European markets.[21] The vast oil reserves, refining capability, ports, and proximity to Europe put Libya in a position not only to fund its own development and security, but also to serve as a strategic ally and energy supplier to world markets. A stable Libya not only provides a buttress against Iranian actions in the Persian Gulf but also contributes to increased energy supplies to world markets and price stability with its Mediterranean deep water ports, and vast stores of high quality crude.

In addition to energy resources, Libya has excellent potential for increased job creation through tourism. Libya is at the cross roads of ancient Mediterranean culture and is home to five UNESCO World Heritage Sites.[22] These sites, which date mainly to the height of the Roman Empire, have remained basically free of damage through the revolution. However experience in both Iraq and Afghanistan shows that the greatest risk to historic artifacts can be post conflict when there are numerous armed groups and little governance. Located on the Mediterranean and close to Port facilities, these World Heritage Sites have excellent potential to help diversify the Libyan economy.

A bit of history may help explain some of the issues facing the new Libya. In ancient times Libya was historically divided into three major regions: Tripolitania, consisting of the area around the modern port city of Tripoli; Cyrenaica, that contains

the majority of know oil reserves and the eastern city of Benghazi; and the Fezzan,

which is mostly desert with few oases and trading routes. Tripolitania is considered part

of the historic Maghreb and has historic and cultural ties to Algeria, Tunisia, and

Morocco. These countries all have lineage and cultural identification with the Berber

tribes of North Africa. The eastern region of Cyrenaica is more closely associated with

the Arab states of the Middle East, especially Egypt. The eastern area of Libya around

Benghazi was largely supported both materially and morally by Egypt during the initial

stages of the anti-Gadhafi uprising and has strong cultural and political ties with Egypt.

The Fezzan mainly encompasses the Sahara region sparsely inhabited by the Tuareg

and Tebu tribes also found in Chad, Algeria, and the Sudan.

Libya is bordered by Egypt to the east; Chad, Sudan and Algeria to the south;

and Tunisia to the west. In the past 40 years, Libya has sought both merger and also

conflict of varying degrees of intensity with each of its neighbors. The most significant

of these conflicts were the Libyan incursions into Chad during the 1970's and 80's.

Libya projected forces into Northern Chad, allegedly to assist Arab tribes in the area,

but also to gain access to mineral deposits rich in Uranium. After numerous successes

and reversals, Libyan forces were finally driven out in 1987 by forces loyal to President

Hissein Habre. Habre was supported by French forces and American arms. The

expulsion of Libyan forces and the capture of vast numbers of Russian produced

armored vehicles and heavy weapons weakened Libya's position as a regional military

power. This conflict also ended Libya's dream of merging the two nations and increasing its direct influence in central Africa. Since the end of war with Chad, relations between the two nations have been amicable.[23]

In the late 1970's, Libya, in response to the Peace Treaty between Egypt and Israel, began to antagonize Egypt. There was a series of marches, border skirmishes, and even a plan for Libyan agents to assassinate the Egyptian President. The United States intervened to forestall Egypt from invading Libya and toppling Ghadaffi. However the Egyptians did manage to destroy dozens of Libyan Tanks, Planes, and Armored Personnel Carriers during a brief border skirmish. Relations between Egypt and Libya have taken a large step forward since the outbreak of the revolution. Egypt provided significant logistical support, safe haven, and refugee assistance, as well as irregular forces to fight alongside the Libyan rebels. With the Egyptian Government also in transition, there is a feeling of good will and solidarity between the two nations. Egypt is looking to play a significant role in the reconstruction and capacity development of Libya subsidized by the international community. If this unfolds, this could be a significant boost to the Egyptian economy and create thousands of jobs[24].

Prior to the revolution, up to a million Egyptians were living and working in Libya. The Egyptian workers are mainly skilled labor that provides the backbone of the manpower to run the oil fields and refineries.[25] It is highly likely that due to the common geography, religion, and cultural ties – a strong relationship will emerge between Egypt and Libya.[26] It is therefore important that a representative, stable, and peaceful Libya emerge from the transition. If Libya is successful establishing a representative and effective new government, it will serve as a positive influence on the fledgling governments in Egypt and Tunisia.[27]

In an article titled <u>The Precarious Economics of the Arab Springs,</u> Robert Springborg contends that the Arab transition to democracy will be long and difficult. He sees the Arab populations as in general too young, too poor, and too insecure to have an effective democratic government. He further contends that Arab countries, including Libya, have a middle class that is too small for the overall population. The work force in the region is poorly educated and lacks both the skilled labor and administrative experience for effective governance.[28]

Springborg contends that successful and sustained democratic transitions occurred in states where the population is balanced and averages over 30 years of age. Economies must have adequate resources, measured by a per capita gross domestic product (GDP) of $6,000 or better. Representative government requires an educated population capable of running effective institutions which can be measured by the Human Capital Development Index. The GDP and education level both depend on sufficient financial resources to fund education, and provide capital to build and operate effective businesses and ventures. Mr. Springborg contends that the youth bulge in the Arab populations, low GDP, and poor education levels make the probability of effective democracy low.

When Springborg's criteria are applied to Libya it suggests that sustained democratic rule is possible. Libya has an average population age of 24, below the mark of 30, but still more balanced than most Arab nations. The National GDP per capita exceeds $6,000, achieving the financial resource threshold required. Indeed Libya, the most advanced nation in the human development index on the African Continent, ranks a respectable 64th in the United Nations Development Program Human Development Report.[29]

A factor not mentioned in Springborg's analysis is nationalism. Libya has a strong sense of national identity as well as a very homogeneous population that is 97% Berber/Arab and Sunni. National identity, economic prosperity, and high human capital development make the formation of a lasting democracy a very viable outcome of the revolution[30]. Outside help in the form of infrastructure investment, technology, and sustained human capital development are still critical requirements for the new Libyan government.

As is the case in Egypt and Tunisia, one time radical and anti U.S. elements such as the Muslim Brotherhood are likely to play a significant role in the initial stages of developing the new Libya and its government. The Mosque and Tribal organizations are the only enduring elements that transcend the Gadhafi regime and will most likely form the basis of the incoming elected government.[31] Those individuals who have been most committed, or radical, and risked the most through the revolution are most likely to fill the leadership positions of the new Libyan Government. This is likely to be a cause of great concern at first, however the burden of responsibility of running the country as well as the presence of secular opposition is likely to quickly moderate the political actions if not the rhetoric in regard to the U.S. and Western allies.[32]

It is likely that China will quickly look to overcome its perception of supporting the Gadhafi regime by seeking trade agreements with the new Libyan Government.[33] China has been active in Africa, Iraq, and Afghanistan and has been willing to assume significant risk in regard to seeking mineral and exploration rights as well as trade

13

agreements and is likely to pursue a similar approach in Libya. Like the U.S., China would benefit from increased supplies of Libyan oil on the world market.

Like China, Russia maintained its support of the Gadhafi regime to the end. This is in large part due to the vast quantities of military sales to the regime. Russia stands to lose more than just military sales from the success of the Libyan revolution. The Greenstream pipeline provides a viable alternative to Natural Gas supplies coming from Russia. Expanding Libyan oil production will only lower prices, pressuring the Russian economy that is also dependant on its export of oil as a significant source of revenue.

Russia is unlikely to actively try and destabilize Libya or the region; however they are likely to be continuously critical of NATO and actions in Libya. Russia will try to create dissention by highlighting civilian casualties caused by NATO, lack of security, as well as any oppression of minority groups in Libya. Russia will also be an obstacle in the United Nations on any resolutions related to Libya or that condemn regimes similar to Resolution 1973. The Russian position on the role of the U.N., and intervention on internal disputes differs greatly from the views of the U.S. Furthermore, Russia is likely in the near future to side with its old allies in Syria and Iran and prevent any future U.N resolution that threatens the current status quo.[34]

The US should pursue a cautious but engaged policy toward Libya that employs military, diplomatic, and economic lines of operation simultaneously. The U.S. must continue to allow Libya to develop its own way forward without the perception of U.S. meddling or interference. The low key approach is low cost and requires limited U.S. resources. As Libya is generally moderate, accustomed to a relatively high standard of living, and in close proximity to Europe; the achievement of U.S. objectives may be attained with limited but well executed diplomacy to include limited economic and security assistance. The current U.S. economic crises as well as ongoing commitments to Iraq, Afghanistan, Israel, and Egypt diminish the probability of large scale economic aid for Libya, no matter how pro western the NTC government may be. The U.S. must be cautious not to make commitments that cannot be fulfilled or even create the perception that there will be large scale U.S. government investment.

Throughout this campaign NATO has been the lead agency in the enforcement of the no fly zone, arms embargo, and protection of civilians. The U.S. has been an active partner in a supporting, as opposed to lead role. Continued U.S. involvement as part of NATO, the UN or other multilateral agency would be well advised at this point. The national interests of the U.S. as it relates to Libya are shared by most of Europe as well as the Arab Gulf States. By continuing in a supporting role, and keeping our footprint confined to participation as part of a coalition, we not only reduce risk and cost to the United States, but enable the strengths of our coalition partners as well. This quiet leadership approach is less likely to inflame anti American or anti colonialism sentiments

The U.S. policy on Libya must also be synchronized with the U.S. policies toward Tunisia, and Egypt, as well as Syria. We must reassure our friends in the region that we are not on a crusade for democracy. The U.S. policy is to act as part of a recognized multilateral agency such as the UN or NATO, to protect the innocent, promote stability and rule of law in the region according to international law. The kingdoms of Saudi Arabia, Jordan, and Qatar could play a critical role and potentially provide essential resources in the stabilization and development of the Maghreb as well as Egypt, and should not be threatened by U.S. actions.

The U.S. should facilitate allied Arab militaries in their efforts to partner with the new Libyan Army with the goal of establishing a professional and competent military. The U.S., working through NATO and its Arab allies can also spearhead the training effort of the new Libyan security forces. Egypt, Qatar and the United Arab Emirates possess sophisticated weaponry, highly trained Special Forces, and a close alliance with the United States and NATO. Each nation took an active role in supporting the NTC by contributing cash, combat sorties (Qatar and UAE only), and likely special operations troops on the ground. The U.S. can continue to play a supporting role as Arab allies take the forefront in training Libyan security forces. Egypt is especially interested in forging close ties with the new Libyan security forces as its military has economic interests in future development and reconstruction activities.[35]

U.S. actions in Libya have been multilateral and part of NATO since the passing of UN Security Council Resolution 1973. Understanding that Europe has both the most to gain and the most to lose in the outcome of the new Libyan government, the U.S. can continue to play a supporting role and wait for the right time to exercise greater influence if needed. The multilateral, diplomacy centered approach is lower cost and relatively low risk when compared with the alternative of direct U.S. military engagement.

Thus far the U.S. would appear to have executed almost perfectly in Libya based on the lessons learned in Iraq and Afghanistan. The Libyan uprising has not been hijacked by a Western "hero", nor has U.S support delegitimized the Libyan Transitional

Government.   Egypt may be the most strategically important nation in the Middle East; however Libya is better positioned to help the recovering U.S. and world economies due to its ability to provide increasing amounts of high quality energy to world markets. Libya can be a positive influence on Egypt and significantly contribute to the economic development and security of Sub Sahara Africa.

As is evidenced by Dr Jabril and Dr Keib leading Libya through the uprising and the establishment of a transitional Government, the greatest U.S. contribution to the future success of Libya likely will not be through the exercise of military power. The U.S. would be well served to continue to educate the current and future leaders of Libya. The Humphrey Fellowship, Legislative Fellows, International Leader Visitor and the Fulbright Programs run by the Department of State are examples of programs already underway that can educate Libyan leaders while hopefully developing mutually beneficial ties to the United States.

In a similar vein to the State Department, the U.S. military can support the education and skill building mission as well.   The most capable Libyan military officers should be offered the opportunity to attend professional education courses in the U.S. at the operational and strategic levels. The utilization of U.S. Special Forces to conduct Foreign Internal Defense Training could also be pursued. With a small number of inconspicuous U.S. Special Forces on the ground in training and advisory roles operating jointly with Libyan security forces, existing weapons depots, WMD stockpiles, and other critical facilities can be quickly assessed and secured if necessary. Risks associated with this option include the presence of U.S. ground forces inciting an Iraq style insurgency, higher cost, and potential loss of additional Libyan as well as

17

American lives. If this action is conducted multilaterally, with special operations forces from Muslim as well as Western nations, this could be very effective with much less risk.

Through mostly multilateral efforts as well as well timed bilateral engagement, the U.S. can maintain a practical approach while avoiding Libya becoming a failed State. Libya can be inhospitable to terrorism and retain control of its borders while preventing the movement of Terrorists and weapons into or out of the country from potentially destabilizing the region.[36] WMD known to be in Libya's possession can be secured. Libya can not only continue to be a major energy supplier to world markets, but expand its current production capacity to promote stable prices and supply of energy in support of the growing world economy.

The utilization of Libyan natural resources will not only fund development in Libya but provide economic opportunity for the poverty stricken sub Sahara African nations on Libya's borders. Remittances by Niger citizens working in Libya is a main source of income for the landlocked nation. Workers that fled the violence of the uprising are returning as security improves in Libya. Chad is aiming to utilize the port facilities in Benghazi as opposed to Douala, Cameroon in order to decrease transportation distance and cost for both imports and exports[37].

The Greenstream pipeline literally and figuratively ties Libya to Europe. This critical infrastructure in not only a critical energy supply for Europe but is soon going to be a cornerstone to capturing the vast and currently wasted natural gas supplies of North Central Africa. The U.S. does not need to fund or even design the development of the Libyan Infrastructure but rather support security and stability efforts that will result in increased private investment. The U.S. must however be ready to provide training and assistance in the areas of developing an elite security force, a professional national Military, and rule of law when requested by the Libyan Government.

Libya posses the critical components required to successfully develop a functioning and lasting democracy. The comparatively high levels of human development, infrastructure, natural resources, national identity, homogeneous population, and ties to Europe make a successful transition probable. The benefit of Libyan success will be felt in the U.S. economy as well as across North Africa and Europe. In addition, Libya can positively influence Egypt; the U.S.'s critical ally on the African Continent. The systems and programs needed to enable Libyan success from a diplomatic perspective are already in place within the U.S. Department of State and should be utilized. The U.S. Armed Forces are more than capable of meeting the training assistance requirements in Libya if tasked. The opportunity to create a lasting ally that can positively influence a strategic area and our critical Egyptian allies must not be overlooked.

Endnotes

[1] Barack H. Obama, "Remarks by the President in Address to the Nation on Libya," (Washington, DC: The White House, March 28, 2011)

[2] Ibid

[3] Ibid

[4] Ibid

[5] Slobodan Lekic, "NATO: Libya action shows Europe's commitment," October 14, 2011, *Associated Press*, http://www.armytimes.com/news/2011/10/ap-libya-actions-shows-europes-commitment-101411/ (accessed March 20, 2012)

[6] Matthew Lee and Raf Cassert, "U.S: Libya Role to Remain Limited Despite Setbacks," April 12, 2011, *The Huffington Post*

[7] Central Intelligence Agency – The World Factbook, https://cia.gov/library/publications/the-world-factbook/geos/ly.html, (accessed March 18, 2012)

[8] Barack H. Obama, "Remarks by the President in Address to the Nation on Libya," (Washington, DC: The White House, March 28, 2011)

[9] Fox News, "Libya's Deadliest Weapons Not Yet Controlled", August 23, 2011, http://www.foxnews.com/politics/2011/08/23/libyas-dealiest-weapons-not-yet-controlled , (accessed March 18, 2012)

[10] Associated Press, "New Libyan PM was Alabama professor for 20 years". http://www.boston.com/news/education/higher/articles/2011/11/01/new_libyan_pm_was_alabama_professor_for_20_years/, (accessed March 19, 2012).

[11] Ibid

[12] Chatham House Middle East and North Africa Program: Libya Working Group Report, *"Libya: Policy Options for Transiton,"* (London, UK, Chatham House August 2011), 5

[13] The Tripoli Post, "Libya: Trash Crisis Engulfs Interim Government in Tripoli, Exposes Its Weakness", March 16 2012, http://www.tripolipost.com/articledetail.asp?c=1&i=8029&archive=1, (accessed March 19, 2012)

[14] "Exiles From Libya Flee to Egypt – Double Tragedy for Sub-Saharan Africans*",* International Federation for Human Rights, Paris, France http://www.fidh.org/IMG/pdf/libyeegypt565ang.pdf, Page , (accessed March 19, 2012)

[15] Chatham House Middle East and North Africa Program: Libya Working Group Report*, "Libya: Policy Options for Transition,"* 6

[16] Anthony Cordesman, *"The Military Balance in the Middle East,".*(Westport, CT: Praeger Publishers), 13-14

[17] "Global Conflict Trends"*,* Center for Systemic Peace, Vienna, VA www.systemicpeace.org/conflict.htm (accessed March 18, 2012)

[18] *"Libya Energy Data, Statistics, and Analysis – Oil, Gas, Electricity, Coal,"* U.S. Energy Administration, http://www.eia.gov/countries/cab.cfm?fips=LY, (accessed March 18, 2012) 1

[19] Ibid, *3*

[20] Ibid, 4

[21] Ibid, *6*

[22] United Nations Educational, Scientific, and Cultural Organization, World Heritage Centre, "*World Heritage List,*" http://whc.unesco.org/en/list (accessed March 18, 2012)

[23] Global Security.org, "Libyan Intervention in Chad 1980-1987", http://www.globalsecurity.org/military/world/war/chad.htm, (accessed March 19, 2012)

[24] Sara El-Essawy, "Arab Spring may turn page in Egypt-Libya Economic Relations*", Al Ahram Daily* (Cairo, Egypt) November 8, 2011

[25] Ibid

[26] Ahmed Eleiba, "Libya Looks to Egypt for Support," *Al Ahram Daily* (Cairo, Egypt) September 5, 2011

[27] Ibid

[28] Robert Springborg, "*The Precarious Economics of Arab Springs,*" *Survival*, 53:6, 85-104

[29] United Nations Development Programme, "Human Development Reports 2011", http://hdr.undp.org/en/statistics/ (accessed March 20, 2012)

[30] Daniel Hannan, Speech to European Parliament, January 19, 2011 http://www.youtube.com/watch?v=5Zj6e4v_sMs, (accessed March 19, 2012)

[31] Kerry Picket, "U.S. recognized Libyan government working with Muslim Brotherhood?," *Washington Times*, August 22, 2011

[32] Robert S. Leiken and Steven Brooke, "*The Moderate Muslim Brotherhood,*" Foreign Affairs Journal, March/April 2007

[33] Steven Sotloff, "China's Libya Problem*"*, March 14, 2012, *The Diplomat Online*, http://the-diplomat.com/china-power/2012/03/14/china%E2%80%99s-libya-problem/, (accessed March 19, 2012)

[34] Howard LaFranchi, "*A cold-war?US-Russia relations falter over Libya and Syria"*, Christian Science Monitor, March 3, 2012

[35] Ahmed Eleiba, "Libya Looks to Egypt for Support," *Al Ahram Daily* (Cairo, Egypt), September 5, 2011

[36] Billie McTernan, "Libya: Welcome to the neighbourhood*," The Africa Report Online*, http://www.theafricareport.com/index.php/201110175175560/news-analysis/libya-welcome-to-the-neighbourhood-5175560.html, (accessed March 19, 2012)

[37]The Tripoli Post, *"Libya can be Chad's Best Trade Corridor,"* October 24, 2010, http://tripolipost.com/articledetail.asp?c=2&i=5025&archive=1, (accessed March 19, 2012)